DEAR LEADER

DAMIAN ROGERS

COACH HOUSE BOOKS, TORONTO

first edition

Published with the generous assistance of the Canada Council for the Arts and the
Ontario Arts Council. Coach House Books also acknowledges the support of the
Government of Canada through the Canada Book Fund and the Government of
Ontario through the Ontario Book Publishing Tax Credit.

LIBRARY AND ARCHIVES CANADA CATALOGUING IN PUBLICATION

Rogers, Damian, author
        Dear leader / Damian Rogers.

Poems.
Issued in print and electronic formats.
ISBN 978-1-55245-308-7 (pbk.)
        I. Title.

PS8635.0425D43 2015   C811'.6   C2014-908027-1

Dear Leader is available as an ebook: ISBN 978 1 77056 413 8

Purchase of the print version of this book entitles you to a free digital copy. To claim
your ebook of this title, please email sales@chbooks.com with proof of purchase or
visit chbooks.com/digital. (Coach House Books reserves the right to terminate the
free digital download offer at any time.)

For the ones
yet to come

ONE

TWO

THREE

FOUR

Say oh leader of the lost
    promise me the company
of the dark,   oh the passing
            smell, the shimmer of evil oh
    it grows like a snake
        moves like the strongest
most beautiful dream in the world

– Joanne Kyger

ONE

FROM THE WINDOWS THE ALLEY

Some days
I'm not on.
I hide inside
the city.
Someday I'll say
thank you
for your invitation
to come see
the pilot whales
skim the coast
of Cape Breton.
Don't tempt me.
I'm working
this summer
on inventing
the life I am
already living.
It takes practice
to see myself
without a mirror.
The ivy leaps over
the fence.
Next year
will be different.

THE NEW MONUMENTS

I was born with the head of an owl and the eyes of a cat.

The ninth abandoned palace of the marquise was like a velvet-lined meth lab.

I learned later she wasn't real royalty, just an out-of-work actress.

I'm not used to living with so little sleep.

Sleep is what keeps me from seeing things straight.

I don't want to go on forever, exactly like this, always a Damian.

Where is the better party you are going to now?

Maybe there will be no grandchildren playing in the long grass.

If you insist on standing up there, at least remove that marble hat.

When he was 38 years old, he found himself
in a stranger's basement confronted by a calendar
that stopped dead on the day he was born.

When he was full grown, he bought snow
tires, was tender to houseplants, sang
to his son about apples all afternoon.

Many years ago, he climbed to the top
of an important Mexican pyramid
that is now closed to tourists.

He had almost no interest in gods, thinking
their existence beside the point. Though he loved
the desert, he had no real plans to live there.

Let's keep wasting our lives and burn
our trash as we go. Some say you don't miss
your water until your well runs dry, but I bet

there's always something else to drink,
even if it's dust. All this chatter about how to be
a man, as if there were some alternative.

Everything we've done is for the best.
Consider the cosmology of Cracker Jack.
The corn was here before you.

TURN YOUR WINDOWS ON

Fill the clawfoot with too much hot water.

Unscrew the light bulbs they say will kill us.

Open the refrigerator and empty its contents into the stove.

Slice eye slits into a quince and hang her head up to dry.

Wallpaper the bedroom with the funny pages.

Lock your hair up in pink plastic curlers and learn to swing a
    rolling pin.

Invite the poorly dressed representatives of boring religions in for a
    game of darts.

Blow out your speakers playing various versions of 'Whiskey in the Jar.'

Buy a condemned movie theatre in Benton Harbor with your credit card.

Rename your pets after the neighbours and call them in for dinner
    from the porch.

Replace your curtains with tinfoil to trap the light inside.

I walked to the corner vegetable store
with its glorious bounty and bottled tea.
I walked past the post office twice forgetting to send
that package on my desk to a new friend.
I haven't listened to a record in weeks.
I'm worried I've made too many mistakes.
I wish I'd bought that book of Li Po poems I didn't buy.
Tomorrow I will have croissants and coffee
and learn the names of the lucky winners.
Have you talked to the doctor? The paperwork
is unfinished. You didn't fill the forms out right.
When I interviewed André, he was painting a mask
from memory. When he finished, his face was green
and he wore a ceremonial cape with an elfin hood.
People are partying down the street in defiance of spring snow.
Everything you're afraid will happen already has.

ODE TO A ROLLING BLACKOUT

Teachers in Oklahoma seek to stop students
from discovering the gateway of digital drugs.

We're all having a hard time, but some problems
are preferable to others: the problems of the very rich,

for example. Some swear the pile is the only known
enemy of the hole. O pretty girls tripping on night,

enjoy this next round, as your pupils pour out
past last call. One of you will soon stop caring

for your hair and your delicates will start to sour.
You will pick your teeth clean with your coke nail.

Now you crackle like a coal, lips slick with petroleum.
Little pots of hot pink clink like crystal as you travel

down the black tube toward morning. Did you kiss
the devil's ass in the alley? Please, no more questions.

STORM

The lake
exchanged
secrets
with clouds
low as light
sockets and
I was radiant
with rage
stuck be-
tween stages:
rapturous
congestion,
an electric web
in my head.
From a back
seat I beamed
the streetcar
through traffic
as rain fell like
power cables.
Sparks splashed
off the sidewalk;
a bright strobe
flashed be-
hind my eyes.
The road rose
in the sky

with no end
in sight.
We live in
the arteries
of a large
ugly animal
and I saw
it move.

A SHOCKING NUMBER OF LOCAL POETS WORK FOR THE INFINITY NETWORK

I'm taking a serious five
   in an office break room,
      admiring my blue willow teacup,

listening to opera
   on my pocket phone.
      The Brazilian soprano's voice

climbs like a vine to the higher
   chambers of her father's mansion,
      where ladies in white gloves, pussies

muzzled under petticoats,
   smooth their skirts. I wonder how she
      wore her hair at home

in the morning, when no one was
   watching. I heard Chuck Berry say
      he sang about school, cars and little

girls so the American babies would buy it.
   He saw a coffee-coloured Cadillac.
      I eye a cobalt carp.

Every day I pass by life's great dramas,
   the kind you'd love to hear about,
      as if they have nothing to do with me.

YOU CANNOT SHED THE DIFFICULT, MOST STUBBORN ASPECTS OF YOUR NATURE WITH ONE DOSE

I don't like to count all my young loves,
pet names buzzing into the ether. I fly
in my dreams, a skill I've hid despite
the light feeling it gives me. I bear this blank
face around town like a dare. Okay, truth:
I burned an early memory on my desk at home.
Okay, that might be a lie, like the one
about how I kissed you goodbye years ago.
In my greenest life, I was a child with a parrot
on my head. Little Pearl lost in the wood.
Little Pearl lost. My eye will go crone in a blink.
Listen to that bee singing of assisted living;
he spirits me safely down a long golden hall.
And you, dear, sent a silver chain for my neck
to help me hit the notes in the grass's secret song
of hush. Hum that tune on your tongue,
haunt me all summer without saying a word.
It's my right to wrap my heart in a riddle.
There is nothing between us that is not love.

I baked a celebrated all-bleached bread ring.

I was trapped in a plane bathroom and we were going down.

I broke into a wealthy woman's house to steal her soap dish.

I kept running late. I kept missing flights to Europe.

I married a man with a moustache and wanted out.

I felt unbeautiful in a fixable way.

I discovered my name sewn into a stranger's sweater.

A man at the food court pressed his thumb into my abdomen.

A woman who felt insufficiently admired cut off her hair.

I sat on a patio with failed approximates of old friends.

My cats loitered outside the Horseshoe Tavern.

Someone said, 'Your mother's house has white mice.'

Then a giant black beetle crawled onto the street flexing its wings.

How many times must I learn the lesson of compression?
Let go of everything you know and start from scratch.
One friend performing backbends on a beach while another
snaps his tibia on an icy patch of Saskatchewan. I don't think
I'm suffering, my days a series of unexpected gifts punctuated
by a blast of the family rage shot deep into my soft plexus.
It occurs to me I don't have to be so many people. If you're staying
alive spinning stories, it's suddenly a skill that you talk too much.
I'm not sure it's smart to unlock the portal. The reformed raver
claimed he saw my inner wheels spin. Red Cloud, are there wars
where you are? Your great-great-grandson appeared on *Democracy
Now!* with a plan. Will my generation be remembered for anything
I haven't forgotten? They mine the hills for gold, they mine the hills
for uranium, and all around the world, columns are cracking.
I've watched you soar all day. Please teach me how you do that.

PRIVATE ROAD MEETS MAJOR INTERSECTION

I skipped through cities where poets leaned into microphones
as their scarves braided together into a trailing batik creek
banked by patchouli-bearing trees. Blackbirds trailed me
down the 401 forming the five Platonic solids over the power lines
as I talked non-stop from Montreal to a farm in Kendal.
We ate scraps from the dinner Kate cooked for a CanCon
icon: maple-dressed salmon, potato mash, watercress salad.
Smoke hopped mouth to mouth in a room with more guitars
than hands to play them. We sang ballads from when denim men
were kings. The radio reported footsteps in the costume room,
unknown bones below the floor, but I believed we were safe inside.
The grand man fused into the easy chair, became one with wind.
We were warm, the walls lined with barnboard, the windows
cloaked in quilts. Later, I gazed upon Orion's Belt and gave
each star a name: Ecclesiastical, Podcast and Anathema.
I was alone with the hunter, out there in the air.

THERE'S NO SUCH THING AS BLUE WATER

I've been thinking that montage is a mental technique
for accepting unity as a convulsive illusion. I feel sick.
I hate it when my stories have holes, though I suspect
there's where the truth leaks out. So go back to bed.
Maybe it's laziness, maybe the delivery system is flawed.
If the gods are making a movie, I've spent years sneaking out
for smoke breaks between takes. I do violence to myself.
I imagine the ones I love dead in their favourite chairs,
dead in distant car crashes. Who are those girls who wear
lipstick to watch TV? The women I know go shut-in,
sleep in their clothes for days in a row. A self-help author
revealed to me with great confidence that life is swinging
from branch to branch in a fog. And I thought, of course
he's right, of course, he's wrong. Let's say we are always
at Point A. From space, the ocean is only a mirror.

TWO

Four-leaf clover (found where?)
folded in paper.

Perfume from France, bottle
blue as a new bruise.

Hand-carved sandalwood box:
white shell   red felt.

Tiny dried seahorse.
Tiny dried sea.

We toured the facility, a woman
    named Jane hovering at the end
        of a corridor, her face

a drained lake. Mother made a wish
    for a room by the border,
        a cat and a job

with health insurance.
    We offered a coin
        to the Falls, left our knives

inside the house. If you
    creep out in the night,
        please bring me back

breakfast, fresh water, the news.
    In the vapours, a vision:
        three of us in one bed

as if we were all in love.
    In this fast catastrophe
        anything is possible: a safe

place with clean carpet,
    an uprush of steam from the red metal
        kettle, a baby girl,

        her head made of wood.

SACBE

I'm discovering
old mysteries
in upstate
New York
while spending
more time
with my mother.
In Mexico
I found
a snakeskin
on the
old road
from Uxmal
to Kabah,
eroded as
the pathways
connecting her
control centres.
Her last letters
contained
the names
of vanishing
species.
I built a box
to keep the
snake's
shed cells

coiled like
a staircase
too fine
to climb.

On Wednesday, Mother gave me a list
    of impossible tasks:
        burn the emperor's passport,

levitate the Pentagon,
    make love not money.
        Don Juan is exhausted

by the action in his lucid dreams.
    For weeks he darts into hands
        unattached to the woman

he loves. My buddies line up
    at the bar, designing their next
        disasters. It grows dark.

The drummer fills with doubt.
    I slide into the smoking circle.
        A crust forms at the edges

of our friendships.
    I'm at the centre of the never-
        ending night.

        You pull me out.

Not all rocks
    are alive. Or
        so I've read.

Someone I love
    is struggling, her thoughts
        a coral net.

The pills fail.
    Her chakras shatter.
        I want to show her

the Canadian Shield.
    I'm in Sudbury.
        It's snowing.

The pine trees looked
    lovely as I drove
        the treacherous roads.

I'm ill-equipped
    for this. I sit
        by a fake fireplace

that frames a real flame.
    I've been crossed
        by two crows today.

THE CHAMELEON WAS BLACK IN THE
LONG WINTER NIGHT

In room 220 she drags
her chair before the door

to lock out the snakes
who steal her toilet paper.

After dinner she swallows
the sun just like winter

eats up August. She opens
her eyes: the sky retreats.

Never will the chair
turn away its love, though

a slithering whisper
slides under the door.

She hides the phone, an old
electric bill, her brush.

You bring soap, clean
towels she won't touch.

Not that you're there.
You're not there.

Owl is a bird, so is raven, crow, but golden phoenix
is something else: vision of giant wings, baby body.
This is an experiment – as is everything we ever try
to do – and I'm learning that though each letter can
count – every space, every single breath through the
throat a block, a vast, snow-white calendar square –
nothing is equal. 'You can't make the lines lie down
like that,' she says with a laugh and I love her but
what do you do with a muse with no view of *l'avenir*?
There's no room for questions, only a memory of blue
satin scraps cut from a dress that dusted the stairs
and the wish to force an idea to conclusion in form.
So I find myself here at the close of the poem, alone
while her voice slips through the bars of this page.

GOOD DAY VILLANELLE

You ran naked out the door.
The neighbours laughed; I chased you down.
I hardly see you anymore.

I know you're busy.
Did I tell you when you were little how
you ran naked out the door?

You got halfway down the street
before I caught you in my arms.
I hardly see you anymore.

I think I told you this before:
I was giving you a bath and then
you ran naked out the door.

It happened fast.
The neighbours laughed.
I hardly see you anymore.

You have to watch a baby close.
I remember once –

You ran naked out the door.
I hardly see you anymore.

BAD DAY VILLANELLE

I swallowed something hard and dark.
It wasn't food. It moves around.
The doctor wants to cut it out.

I feel it now it's on my hip.
It's very painful when it shifts.
I swallowed something hard and dark.

I'm telling you
it's money that
the doctor wants. To cut it out

will save my life.
I need your help.
I swallowed something hard and dark.

He ran my body through five tests.
Then the doctor told me straight.
I'll die if they don't cut it out.

I'm telling you it has to go.
There is no medicine that works
on something quite this hard and dark.
The only road is cut it out.

CURSE

You who shoved the orphan down on the candy-striped mattress.

You who fed the aged radioactive scraps, served
sunny cheese singles cut with chemical waste.

You who poisoned the river for a better seat at the picture show.

You who lured the animals into the theme park.

You who sell tickets to the crossfire.

You who say we will not be eaten alive.

Your children will unbraid your bloodline
while you scrape in service of the wrong snake,
cracking your pickaxe on a golden orb of protection.

Insects will nest in your spider-veined flesh
as pinworms populate your plumbing.

Look at your works, you asshole, and despair.

The report is marked by a conspiracy of cruelty,
and is written in a style suited to the spreadsheet.

Thank your boss for the favour he has bestowed on you
by entrusting to you the mission of casting us overboard.

Through the sea's green lens, I see your future shrink.

Everything you do to her, your children will do to you.

Your children will seal you behind a soundproof door.

Your children.

LA BELLE INDIFFÉRENCE

I found a photograph –
my hair was blond!
Then we played cards.

It was enjoyable. Every-
one here is very nice.
I found a photograph

of you and someone else
outside my house in Florida
where we played cards.

They came to paint
our nails for free.
I found a photograph

of you as a tiny baby.
How is the darling boy?
Can he play cards?

I can't seem to sleep.
I went to bed and dreamed
of a photograph,
a pack of playing cards.

CONDITIONAL

This is the letter where I explain
how you are a unit of composition.

It's Friday night on the Queen car, passengers
plugged into the promise of potential parties.

A woman in red tights carries a record crate and a bag
that reads: I'M SORRY I'M SORRY I'M SORRY GOODBYE.

For your farewell you filled eight notebooks
with the names of interesting animals.

Humming an old song:
You need me; you're gone. (×2)

If you forgive me for changing seats.
If you forgive me for swearing at the driver.

If you forgive me for carrying my brain
in my head like a glass of black water.

A Siberian husky sits with me as his drunk
owner calls commands from the front.

I can't believe my luck. But the wolf
doesn't love us. He trots off.

In your sleep, I hear you repeat:
I don't want you to follow me.

MRS. FRANK LLOYD WRIGHT'S BLACK LAMBSWOOL COAT

And we were talking about house
    parties where all the guests
        try to describe
            the milky void   behind the sky, or

offer advice on how to soothe
    the Spirit of the Angry Stovetop.
        (Sauté the plantain weed that works
            its way out through the cracks

in the cement squares out back.)
    By the bottles, a man with a yellow
        mark on his heart demands,
            Do you paint your toenails?

Do you move your body to fast music
    in order to build a more beautiful
        outline?
            What do you, little dove, do?

What he means is   *Forgive me*   *my inabilities.*
    Don't laugh at his public loss of vitality,
        the shrunken head trapped in his knapsack.
            Please don't call me sick, or a sad sack of shit.

Tell your own story. Say an eagle kept pace
    with your car as you rode along the Niagara River.
        Say you're a poet. Maybe you mean
            Hi, I have a lot of feelings.

THREE

Found delirious on the streets of Baltimore. Died days later.
Shipwreck at the age of 40.
Typhoid fever. 44.
Orphaned at 14, dead from tuberculosis at 25.
Lost at 27 on a French hospital ship anchored in the Aegean Sea.
Sister stabbed mother to death in a fit of anxiety.
Drowned at the age of 30.
Worked at the post office until death at 37.
Died of fever in Greece on way to war.
Went down sailing at age 29.
Died of pneumonia while commanding a hospital in Boulogne.
Stabbed to death in bar fight.
Killed in action one week before war ended.
Asylum.
Drank to death.
Jumped off an ocean liner.
Overdosed on sleeping pills.
Drowned swimming in Lake St. Clair in August.
Sick with Graves's Disease for many years. Died of breast cancer.
Small pox.
Swallowed by a sudden storm after seeing Doppelgänger.

POEM FOR ROBIN BLASER

O I know your thoughts are with the gods,
so young and loose.

I sit still and watch you materialize, as your ring –
the eye of your hand – checks me out.

I feast on your approval;
my erased attachment attracts it.

The sun rolled over White Sands National Park,
a wedding dance on the trackless dunes of my design.

You see all are tamed
out of our chains   in this way:

light freezes into cubes   for our cocktails,
        atmospheric gases are trapped   on their planets.

I must keep my feet on the floor
if I'm ever to achieve your speed.

You blew smoke at me and smiled.
Nothing is   so easy.

THE PERFORMER SPEAKS TO HER PERFECT
APPRENTICE BENEATH THE ARCHES

Step one: understand the universe.
The trick is to slip into a trance, to stay
in a somnambulant state while smiling.

Do a little soft-shoe. Bend your head.
Then excavate the audience for parts.
Get in there and eat their hearts out.

But don't listen to me. I remember
a time when fame was not particularly
prized, though stages were reserved

for the fearless. It was us against them
back then. Now I don't know. I want
to go home and study the viscous slick

on the surface of my coffee before I quit.
Take my face paint and hot plate, finish
the dish of small fruits in the freezer.

I'd like it if we could be friends. Friend,
please give me time to gather my gear.
I never believed they'd see me leave.

JUNE 20, 2012

Witching hour. Lightning bugs.
I accidentally crushed
a coyote skull today
beneath my boot. Fur
and bones drying in the broomsedge
by the road, under a pretty hill.

We were looking for him
and he found us.

Good morning, Wolfe Island. You set the scene with little cakes,
coffee pot and fruit plate. No one loves a bummer in the summer.
I chose to go-go-go in the town square.

A lost crop of kids waited behind the club for the Good Humor Man.
He sees everything they need and it's his good business to sell it.

I look up from my breakfast spread to see a bright spider hanging
in front of my face. He's happy to live and let live if I am.

A would-be despot knows that the mountain
will never be fooled, but maybe the people will be.
The times are always open to interpretation.
He dreams of a red telephone that will only ring for him.

If we're lucky, he'll die an old man in a garden guarded
by a cheap cherub, a witness by the water treatment.

Welcome to the daily planet, says the spider,
finding no frame upon which to hitch his home.

On the highway, a hawk circles the van and the shoulder
gravel gives way to road flowers: Purple Paintbrush,
Dry River Rushes, Exploding White Allergen.
And more and more and more again.

A house is not a hotel, which is what makes
staying at a B&B so awkward.

By the ferry, children chased their dog
around a decorative anchor. As we drove away,
we felt alone again. Or we didn't.

POEM FOR DEATH

'Politicians, in my eyes, ruin our best chances
of making this work,' said the man running for mayor.

Once they wondered, 'Where do we go from here?'
And here is as far as they got.

'If I start freaking out over this spill, I'll never stop,'
said the oil can. 'I want to get back to my wife.'

'You're a prisoner,' said the snow leopard to the bank teller.
'You'll be the last of our kind to be free.'

'Let the world turn,' said the witch,
'as if it would do so without you.'

'That feels amazing,' said the rock 'n' roll victim,
as he bled from his head. 'Do it again.'

What can I say? I can't wait to meet the future beasts that keep
on knocking from the other side of that big red door.

THE WARLOCK'S FORELOCK

This rain reminds me how I fell
in love with steel drums as a girl

in Detroit's Hart Plaza, wanted to hear
that patterned ting-ping-ping all day,

while brushing my teeth, while reading
my horoscope in the *Free Press*,

while unpacking a packed lunch.
My son's father pours me a glass

of terrible wine. We joke it has notes
of strawberry, rhubarb and lake trout.

I watched a decades-old documentary
in which the author's father handled

hemlock on an island outside Ottawa.
My father tells me I'm his greatest

regret. He means not knowing me (one
hopes). It reminds me of a dumb song.

My son is asleep after drinking from me
too soon after I consumed that bad booze.

When I was 22 I drank a bottle of rosé
and zonked out under a tree beside

the intended tent. I was in a campground
in Menton. France. That's all I remember.

Also: the English girls I travelled with didn't
much love museums. Did I see Jean Cocteau's

château? Maybe. My son thinks I'm perfect
when I do nothing but lie silently in a room

feeding him while I try not to dwell
on my mother's bills so that worry won't

pass from my nervous system into his. One
time I drank a rancid mud-thick brew

that made me see snakes in the floor tile.
I thought I was the Virgin Mary, radiant

and swaddled in borrowed white skirts
meant to shield my ovarian vibrations.

We stood up and sat down as we sang
allegedly magical phrases in Portuguese.

One guy saw light shoot out of my head.
Tonight, I tune the rain. Our least-favourite

cat trapped in the worst of it. I felt
love as we rescued him from his tiny

terror. Once he was safe I lost interest.
I cried this afternoon. It's my new thing.

You've been thinking your parents aren't the geniuses they once were. I spent last night watching a man with a Mohawk dance to music made by men in sweat-soaked button-downs. We stood by the banks of a beautiful river and laughed at those more fortunate than ourselves. Together we could write a best-selling novel, the kind they display in wire racks at the food store. Let's pick up a story and a box of freezer-burned popsicles. The weeds in your backyard irritate me so much more than the ones in mine. The flagstone is splitting and I don't trust you behind the wheel of anything bigger than a Big Wheel. Some of your most treasured possessions are totally bullshit. The greater the humidity, the less kindness I share. Then I remember how much I like how the trees here are taller than the buildings. I know I owe you more than I care to acknowledge. Allow me to buy you a sack full of fruit.

I was listening to someone talking about Auden talking about Bruegel talking about Icarus and the idea of overreaching one's limits to disastrous result while the world whirred on struck me as oddly reassuring. For years I didn't know waxwings were a type of bird. There's so much I still don't know, including the basic mechanics of flight. I don't study contracts even though I know my best interests are betrayed in little print. I went back to high school and all the girls were my friends. But here's the thing: there's no point in shoving a message about the relative value of compassion compared to a diamond chip. You get it or you don't. And yet, I hope it's not too late for me to see a fresh commitment to happiness founded like a colony at the edges of every city. Each movement swells to a certain mysterious digit and then draws back on its own dissent almost overnight. This morning, a zealot raved on the beach. 'When we are one with the water,' he cried, 'there will be no need to wash.'

1   Purple plus sign on a stick
    means I've multiplied.

2   I'm a walking bag of salt water.
    This makes me your first ocean.

3   A woman takes my pulse,
    says, *I think you're having a little girl.*

4   I carry you, little candle, snub of wax,
    like an unlit lantern.

5   Bless us. Now we are four.

6   I read my son a bedtime story
    so much like so many stories:
    a pretty girl marries a rich white bear
    who warns her not to listen to her mother.

7   I'm planning our adventures in Spain
    when I see the first spot.

8   Maybe I'll have a baby in the spring.
    Maybe not.

9   Waiting for my doctor.
    To hear what? Stuff I know?
    Stuff I don't know.

10   Doctor looks down and frowns.

11   Another me stands in front of *Guernica*
     with you ticking inside.

12   Bless us. Now we are three.

13   This goodbye goes slow,
     bleeds for weeks.

     And then, home alone:
     a horror show.

14   He ran upstairs to find me naked from the waist down,
     blood everywhere.

15   At Emergency, I lie down on the floor of the waiting room,
     my hoodie folded under my head.

16   Bless us. Now I am one
     woman on a gurney guided by strangers.

17   Doctor says, *Sometimes it won't let go.*

18   Another me races with new luggage to catch a final flight.
     Another me eats octopus at a bar with a single glass of cold beer.

19   Doctor says, *I know.*
It feels like I'm ripping
your insides out.

20   Another me enters the least touristy flamenco cave in Granada.

21   Doctor says, *I think I got it all.*

22   Rush of morphine.
The instant wish for more.

23   Another me breakfasts on a terrace
overlooking the Alhambra.
Travel guides explain its structure
is one giant repeated prayer.

24   Nurse says, *A lot.*
That was a lot.

25   Nurse says, *Sure, you should go to Spain.*
Get insurance. Doctor says, *No. Pre-existing condition.*

26   Doctor looks down and frowns.
Wash your foot.

27   A line of juniper trees and narrow cedars pointing up,
like so many middle fingers.

28   The women say keep my head warm.
     I sleep in the hoodie, my grim autumn robe.

29   Another me struggles to push my son's stroller
     down cobbled steps and through a hole in the old city wall,
     following the river to the Arabic market.

30   Cancel the plane tickets, the rooms with views.

31   The sitter says, *It was His will.*

32   The other sitter says, *Don't try for another. Why mess with perfection?*

33   I drink nettle. I eat herbal tablets prepared in China.

34   My son cries in his sleep. Settles.
     I sneak rose quartz into the bed.

35   Instead of taking the train out of Madrid,
     I am in an empty hallway back in the hospital,
     following the black line, the peeling black line.

36   Old woman beside me complaining.
     They were supposed to cut my hair and now I'm in the hospital.

37   She coughs her Dark Age plague in my face.

38   *I was here for so many years, believe me.*

39   I snap at the old lady that we all have to wait
     as my neighbour texts to tell me *Only light*
     can pass through your field of light.

40   I write jokes in my head.
     Do you do your face for a D&C?

41   My body stays changed. I text
     a friend about this dead-baby weight.
     A sentence with no.

42   This happens to women all the time.
     People tell me this all the time.

43   In my lonely fog,
     I leave the baby gate open
     at the top of the stairs.

44   In my lonely fog,
     I become a flight of stairs.

45   It's like it never happened.
     Except it takes so long to unhappen.

46   This is not how I planned it.

47   I planned a single cold beer served in a tall glass.
     With octopus. An octopus sandwich.

48   Machines measure the remaining evidence in centimetres.

49   My immortality vanishes.

     The women say, *Don't get wet. Stay warm.*
     Ginger tea. Bone broth, beef stew. Stay in bed.

50   Friends ask, *How was Spain?*

51   They do things differently in other countries.
     From now on I'll live in another country.

52   And I'll always be
     your only ocean.

EXPLAINING ECOLOGY TO MY TWO-YEAR-OLD

This stump
  is what's left
    of the trunk
      of a tree
        that went bye-bye.

IT'S AFTER THE END OF THE WORLD

For Sun Ra

The bandleader seeks the sound of duos: Call. Response.
Lovers bicker back and forth in angelic proclamations.
This is the fight after the finish! Myth Versus Reality! The ideal
of lion versus the scrawny, tawny body she shot on film.
Over the Internet friends send love in every direction. (Myth.)
Science approaches like a metallic mantis. There's a scarab
in the mattress. The Egyptian March drones during a procession
of supersonic pushcarts. Do the Watusi, do the Twist. The dance
moves of Saturn are not for sale. Every childhood is a Black Forest.
(Myth.) Strange dreams in which animals appear as symbols
for other animals. Strange worlds in which we are not also animals.
When the story ends, the screen is black. (Myth.) I see the devil
in the tree across the street. He speaks to me, remotely.
He says it's after the end of the world. What next.

THE CROSSROADS

Old Harry will open his mouth
and invite you in.

Carry a chicken bone, or a lion's paw.
Prepare a pot of hot soup.

Feed him and you're off the hook,
but if he's hungry, things begin

to happen. Be cool. Freeze
your face into a mask.

No matter where you go
there are people of power.

There were a string of kings in Chicago
and I knew a few of them.

There was a group of us
and I wasn't a part of it.

I left. I met the President
of the Middle of the Road.

He wore a T-shirt advertising
rotten food and lousy coffee.

Then the bird of my mind
descended.

The bird of my mind
returned to find

its nest was a mess.
I ingested my ancestors.

144,000 delusional godheads
marched through my radiant inner city.

Now I serve the elders with both hands
and I let the fruit ferment on the branch.

FOUR

As you know, I did not join the Hole in the Universe Gang
or follow Father Yod of the ridiculous robes. I flowed
through my crises beautiful as a bruise, and alone. A man I loved
drove his motorcycle off the fat lip of Big Sur into glittering
oblivion. A new nation of Penelopes practiced the art of the loom,
planting a never-finished forest in which wildflowers bloomed
on the backs of jean jackets and hand-sewn throw pillows,
while I waited for you to choose me. The waitress at the health
food restaurant was a lemon-scented sun to my Death Valley
moon. I swooned as out the window your dark cluster rose
in the sky. How glorious was your shining forth from the horizon
when you detonated the Two Lands with your terrible rays!
I starved till my bones shone, and your voice rang in my ear.

Cocaine is like, whatever, sex sex sex. Hotel sex, public bath-
room sex, no-one-can-come-but-you-fuck-forever sex. Heroin is
a slow deep wet kiss with your own dim reflection without ever
climbing out of the chair to look in the mirror. A guy I liked
described acid as having every drawer and closet door inside
you spring open at once. Pot is unpredictable, sometimes an
ecstatic lift in communion to song, other times the brain eating
itself in an edgy paranoid panic. Booze is a sloppy, ugly, face-
slackening slide toward the grave or at least the gutter, sinking
into the street's shallow pit, shit streaming by you, oblivious.
Pills: a synthetic, efficient bubble, either of energy or apathy or
both. And men, they turn you into a vessel, rowing farther
away with every stroke.

But the Leader, he cleans my hair with his feet.

My memory is with me and it shall not be taken away, for I am
a possessor of memories that make memories. I don't want to forget
a noun. I'll download what we witnessed. Remind me
the day, the year, our planet's name and coordinates. Warning:
don't eat food from another time, it invites toxins into the ship.
In Lemuria, I never paid to run the refrigerator. O Lion, I am
an old handmaiden; I will not lay the pretty baby in the lap
of the impostor, and my memories will not be siphoned from me
by the Administrator. Repel the reptilian who conspires to hide
my memories before I enter the Ocean Unlimited. Get back,
Crocodile of the West, sent to snuff out the words *yellow* and
money! I saw my enemy unhinge his jaw to suck down a kitten.
Please lead me to safe paper, help me write it down right.

Adoration, nocturnal, in the Ocean Unlimited.
Blessed Buffalo Burger, the leader's devotion to.
Board of Health, agents of.
Doctors, absence of.
Humility, the leader's spirit of.
Mortification, the leader's practice of.
'We the people of the shrinking kingdom,' first use;
    see also *Leader*.

YES, I'M A WITCH

For Yoko Ono

There was a storm.
　　When it cleared, the sky said here:
　　　　a half glass of water

to see the seasons through.
　　When I was a little girl, Mother
　　　　said I could be anything.

I said a rabbit.
　　White hare running
　　　　through white air.

I said yes to sleeping in a see-through dress.
　　Yes to a pair of scissors for the people
　　　　to cut holes in my clothes.

I sat there and watched them do it.
　　I looked up in the night
　　　　at the naked moon.

I asked her, *Are you cold?*
　　Do you need a blanket?
　　　　Oh, no, she said. *No, no, no.*

When I awoke I was a mountain.
    And I was the cloud
        floating beside it.

How do we get back down?
    Iron your mind out
        like a crisp bedsheet.

Hang it on a clothesline.
    Call it
        the sky.

SOLAR ECLIPSE

After Helen Adam

A black coin rolls over Ra.
You knock at your mother's door,

ignoring the overgrown hedges.
The sun drops. The sun trembles.

Inside her house that burns with light,
your mother wakes into the elevated

consciousness of childhood. With an astral flash
the sky recedes. This is how your mother breathes.

The door is locked and hot to touch.
You stand on the porch and turn away.

You are not with your mother
in her burning house all night.

DEAR LEADER

Fuck the fourteen-year-old who flirted with my boyfriend. If I've turned ugly on the inside, it's all her fault. Where were you when my love split the planet in two? I knew who would undo me. Did you grab her throat and drag her downstairs? I've been betrayed by the boys who sprayed my name under the overpass, the ones who walked me home in a pack, called me their tender pet. This isn't over yet.

I eat you I eat you I eat you.

I remember a band of beloved wife beaters. We drowned their sound
    with our screams.

I discovered your eye in a smooth wand of Montana agate. Horses
    rained through your pupil.

I hid in an abandoned cliff dwelling where no one could hear me.

I met a bear in the woods. I think I'm still walking backward.

I sewed a soft-sculpture man out of blue cotton. I dressed him in jeans
    and a corduroy hat. You leapt into his lap and squealed, *Daddy!*

I remember Christmas trees crying on the curb.

A green field thick with the ghosts of Civil War soldiers.

To Do lists and meal plans. Beauty regimes built on baby oil and blush.

The boys at school preferred my simple stockings.

I remember the razor my husband bought me before we were married.

The cats and how each one passed.

Your apartment in Chicago with seven dead rats in the crawl space,
    your boyfriend from Princeton.

Paris: rows of roses, a note out of my range.

London: two weeks of beer and bread, the men who saw us as sisters.

I remember reading. So many centuries, so many lines about flies.

REPORT OF THE NIGHT NURSE

I'm not prepared for the
    ceremony. In the office,
        I see the rabbi's husband,

the one who wrote that poem for Pluto.
    Hello! Let's pretend I'm clothed.
        I'm putting on a show.

I make a show of it. Show me
    the schedule for tonight's
        entertainment. Mother's here.

I'm getting married! Come see!
    She's upset. She's
        a bathrobe on the floor.

She wants to comb her hair,
    doesn't want the world
        to see her like this.

The world is getting smaller,
    I say, and more crowded.
        In a way, it's better like this.

DEAR LEADER

I was too timid to be Slime Queen, the beauty who communed
with the soft bubbling scum on someone's lake after lunching
on lysergic acid with a gang of pranksters. The age of gilded
gurus continues on under corporate sponsorship, and still
the comfortable suffer in their well-cut pantsuits. Cruel California
calls out for fresh recruits; killer converts map the continent's
most generative conference centres. Please accept this pamphlet
illustrated with mail-order aura enlargers. Are you illuminated?
At the bottom of the Pacific, microscopic monsters chase every
bioluminescent organism twinkling in the brink. In my youth,
I too was a magnet, and I did not dim for decades. Set adrift,
I learned to shuck my shell, oozing out into the Waters of Truth.
My head shall not be taken from me, my head shall not be taken.

THE BOOK OF GOING FORTH IN GLITTER

See the daughters of the screenshot
        arrange their arms like
                the ladies in major paintings

for an online salon. See them inventory
        their makeup bags in popular verse.
                What's worse? My peeling skin

or how my mind shrivels in its cap?
        A beautiful man who never made middle age
                claimed there would be no TV in the afterlife.

He danced defiantly
        in his underwear
                through the Temple of Night.

Take comfort in your ground-mica mouth, your well-
        documented pout, the kiss you send out
                into orbit. A face to launch a thousand

comments, though who knows what really counts.
        Observe. Measure how much it means
                when a chignon shifts a quarter-inch.

So said Baudelaire. So there.

Some swear you've arrived for your own purposes, but I sensed your
benevolence when you appeared ahead of me in the halls. You want
me to survive. The bald cats messing with the medicine have clipped
my number out of the registry. The Administrator insisted a sitter see me
through my hours of daylight. I know you're higher on the hierarchy
and this keeps me calm. Evil aides sneak into my room after-hours
to hook me up to a drug drip. I wish I never came north; there's seven
feet of snow against the door, not that they let me leave in any weather.
Florida is just a distant smear of sun, the ocean one long wave. I chant
your name, clasping it as an amulet to deflect the great eraser that rubs
its bare feet on my body. On special days, they rustle up gangs of junior
indoctrinauts to sing their lessons listlessly. The only honest eyes belong
to babies and dogs; their gaze opens the gate to the Field of Offerings.

I summon the ghost of the Chevrolet dealership, the one
who drank Rothschild wine and cursed the federal reserve.
Is he revisiting the vines of Vietnam or caressing his cache
of semi-automatics, the collection he kept in case of coup?
He sucked on cinnamon sticks to quit the tobacco products
laced with formaldehyde and battery agents. He loved me
in the little black dress and my ankle-strap heels from Payless.
O my heart, handed down by my mother, fickle and cold.
O my heart of my different ages, do not stand up as a witness
against me in the courtroom. Leader, your deeds are clean
as the whistles I once drew down the street. Bring me he who
would fight the Administrator and that stinking counsel of lies.
Send the Marine to protect me. Let me go forth to happy day.

ACKNOWLEDGEMENTS

Grateful acknowledgement is made to the editors of the following journals, in which some of these poems first appeared: *Boston Review*, *Event*, *Four Way Review*, Hazlitt, Lemon Hound, Likestarlings, *Literary Review of Canada*, Radar Poetry, *Riddle Fence*, *Taddle Creek*, the Toronto Review of Books, the *Toronto Star*, the *Walrus* and *White Wall Review*.

The Joanne Kyger quote that opens the book is from her poem 'Under the Green Light,' which appeared in *All This Every Day* (Big Sky, 1975).

Love and gratitude to all at Coach House Books, especially to Susan Holbrook; Jeramy Dodds; Sarah Smith-Eivemark; and Alana Wilcox, Empress of the Letterpress.

So many roses to Hoa Nguyen for inspiration and support. A closet full of tiger dresses to Lynn Crosbie for same.

Thanks to André Ethier for granting permission to use his beautiful painting on the cover.

Thanks to Amanda Schenk for the photograph and to Ken Mikolowski for letting me borrow his T-shirt.

Impossible without Michael J. Belitsky and Levi Lincoln Rogers Belitsky.

This book was assisted by grants from the Canada Council of the Arts and the Ontario Arts Council.

Damian Rogers is from the Detroit area and now lives in Toronto, where she works as poetry editor of House of Anansi Press and as creative director of Poetry in Voice, a national recitation contest for Canadian high school students. Her first book of poems, *Paper Radio*, was nominated for the Pat Lowther Memorial Award.

Typeset in Albertan.
Albertan was designed by the late Jim Rimmer of New Westminster, B.C., in 1982. He drew and cut the type in metal at the 16pt size in roman only; it was intended for use only at his Pie Tree Press. He drew the italic in 1985, designing it with a narrow fit and a very slight incline, and created a digital version. The family was completed in 2005, when Rimmer redrew the bold weight and called it Albertan Black. The letterforms of this type family have an old-style character, with Rimmer's own calligraphic hand in evidence, especially in the italic.

Printed at the old Coach House on bpNichol Lane in Toronto, Ontario, on Zephyr Antique Laid paper, which was manufactured, acid-free, in Saint-Jérôme, Quebec, from second-growth forests. This book was printed with vegetable-based ink on a 1965 Heidelberg KORD offset litho press. Its pages were folded on a Baumfolder, gathered by hand, bound on a Sulby Auto-Minabinda and trimmed on a Polar single-knife cutter.

Edited by Susan Holbrook
Designed by Alana Wilcox
Cover design by Ingrid Paulson
Cover painting, *Untitled*, by André Ethier, courtesy of André Ethier
        and Derek Eller Gallery, New York

Coach House Books
80 bpNichol Lane
Toronto ON M5S 3J4
Canada

416 979 2217
800 367 6360

mail@chbooks.com
www.chbooks.com